A Kid's Guide

2024

Summer Olympics

Jack L. Roberts and Michael Owens

Curious Kids Press • Palm Springs, CA
www.curiouskidspress.com

A WORD TO PARENTS

Curious Kids Press was founded in 2017 with the goal of providing young readers with fun-to-read books about countries and cultures around the world. Since our founding, we have published 32 different books in our series titled "A Kid's Guide to . . . ." Each full-color book includes dozens of photos and illustrations along with high-interest text, all design to give "curious kids" a better understanding of the world around them.

In addition to our "country books," we have also published several special editions of the "Kid's Guide" series, including *A Kid's Guide to Climate Change*, *A Kid's Guide to Native American Culture*, and *A Kid's Guide to World Religions*, as well as a special edition every two years about the winter or summer Olympics.

This year, we are happy to publish *A Kid's Guide to the 2024 Summer Olympics*. The book provides fun facts and statistics about the 32 sports that will be featured at the 2024 Summer Olympics in Paris, France.

We hope your curious kids (and you, too!) will find *A Kid's Guide to the 2024 Summer Olympics* both informative and entertaining, as everyone gets ready for the exciting Summer Olympics, starting July 26, 2024.

Publisher: *Curious Kids Press, Palm Springs, CA 92264.*
Designed by: *Michael Owens*
Editor: *Sterling Moss*
Copy Editor: *Janice Ross*

Table of Contents

Welcome to the 2024 Summer Olympics

Paris

On Monday April 6, 1896, in Athens, Greece, the king of Greece opened the first Olympic Games of what's called "the modern era."

At those first games, 241 men (no women) from fourteen different countries competed in nine different sports: athletics (track and field), cycling, tennis, swimming, gymnastics, fencing, weightlifting, wrestling, and shooting. (Actually, eleven sports were planned, but yachting and rowing were cancelled on the day of competition due to bad weather and strong winds.)

One hundred twenty-eight years later, the Games of the XXXIII Olympiad will be held in **Paris, France**, from July 26 to August 11. A total of 10,500 athletes from 206 nations (or their territories) will compete in 32 different sports (329 events).

This book introduces all 32 sports that will be contested at the Olympics this summer. You'll read about the history of the sport, some fun (and even bizarre) facts about the events, and what to expect at Paris 2024.

We hope you enjoy this book about the Summer Olympics. It's the world's largest sports celebration of the modern era.

Get Ready For the International Competition of Physical Exercises and Sports
The What?!

The organizers of the modern Olympics didn't actually use the term "Olympics" very often. Instead, they called the sports event the "International Competition of Physical Exercises and Sports." As a result, many athletes never knew they actually competed in the Olympic Games. No wonder.

Just For Fun: A Quick Quiz

Before we jump into the upcoming events, here's a quick one-question quiz about past Summer Olympic events.

Question: Which sport was never an Olympic event?

(1) Tug of War

(2) Squash

(3) Rope Climbing

Did you say "squash"? If so, you're right. This racket-and-ball sport has never been contested at the Olympics.

But the other two have been featured in several modern Olympics.

Tug of War took place at five Olympic Games in 1900, 1904, 1908, 1912, and 1920. Great Britain holds the most gold medals (2) in this sport.

Rope climbing was contested at only four Olympic Games: 1896, 1904, 1924, and 1932. At the first rope climbing event in 1896, the rope was 14 meters high (about 46 feet). Only the two Greek competitors made it to the top.

Neither of these two sports will be contested at the upcoming XXXIII Olympiad in Paris, France. But there will be one *new* sport at the 2024 Summer Games. Do you know what it is? Keep reading to find out.

By the way, here's some good news for squash lovers. The sport will be contested for the first time ever at the 2028 Summer Olympics in Los Angeles, California. We can't wait.

AN Imaginary Interview WiTH tHe FOUNDer OF tHe MODerN OLYMPiCS

Suppose you could talk with **Pierre de Coubertin**, the founder of the modern Olympics, about the history of the modern Games. What questions would you ask? Here are some questions these curious kids wanted to know.

Who was the first athlete to win a medal at the 1896 Olympics?

He was an American, actually—a track and field athlete named James Connolly from Boston. He won for the triple jump (though, back then, it was called the hop, skip, and jump).

How many different sports have been contested at every modern Olympics since 1896?

How many countries have competed at every Summer Olympics since the beginning of the modern Games?

Only five: Four of them included athletics, aquatics, cycling, fencing, and gymnastics. Can you guess the fifth one? I'll tell you later.

Only six. Greece, Australia, France, Great Britain, Italy, and Switzerland.

What event do you think was the most unusual sport ever contested at the early Olympics?

That's an easy one. But you probably won't believe it. The answer is club swinging. It was only held twice—once at the 1904 Olympics in St. Louis, and again at the 1932 Olympics in Los Angeles.

Were there always bronze, silver, and gold medal winners?

So, who won the club swinging event?

Actually, no. It wasn't until the III Olympiad in 1904 that bronze, silver, and gold medals were awarded.

In both 1904 and 1932, Americans crushed the sport. But to be honest, there were only three club swinging competitors at the 1904 Olympics— all Americans and four at the 1932 Olympics, three from the USA and one from Mexico.

What did the winners get before that?

Well, at the 1896 Olympics, the winners got a silver medal and an olive branch. Runners-up got a bronze medal. And here's a fun fact. The 1900 Summer Olympics is the only games in which a rectangular medal was awarded. Here's what it looked like.

So, did you figure out what the fifth sport is that has been contested at every Olympics since 1896? The answer is [drum roll, please] tennis.

WHERE IN THE WORLD IS PARIS, FRANCE?

THE XXXIII OLYMPIAD will be held in Paris, the capital of France. France is located in Western Europe. Its borders touch Germany and Belgium in the north, the Atlantic Ocean in the west, and the Pyrenees mountains and Spain in the south, and the Alps, Switzerland, and Italy in the east. The last time the Summer Olympics was held in Paris was one hundred years ago in 1924.

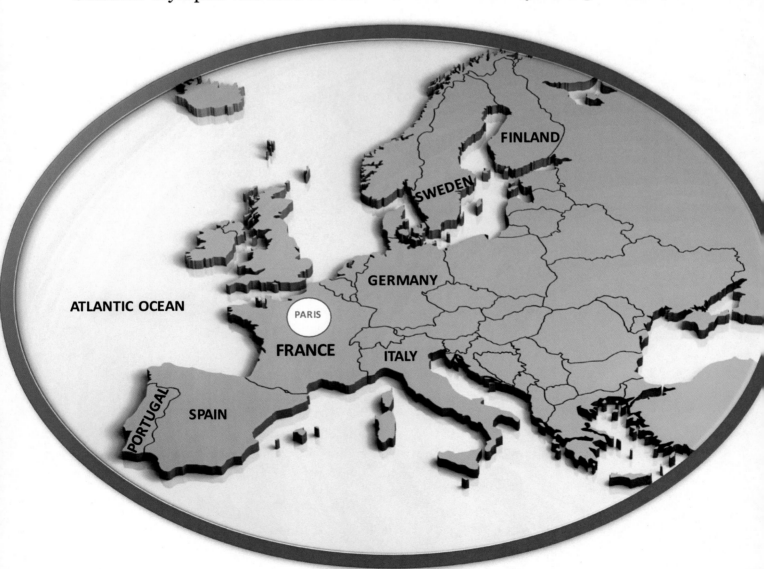

The 32 Summer Olympic Sports

Aquatics

"Aquatics" is the name given to five different water sports at the Olympics. Those five sports include swimming, water polo, diving, artistic swimming, and marathon swimming. Here are some facts about these water sports at the Olympics.

Swimming is one of only five sports that have been contested at every summer Olympic Games since 1896. Women were allowed to compete starting in 1912.

Diving was held for the first time at the 1904 Olympic Games in St. Louis, MO. Only two countries participated in the two diving

2024 Olympic Aquatics At a Glance

Olympic Debut: Swimming, 1896; water polo, 1900; diving, 1904; artistic swimming, 1984; marathon swimming, 2008.

Number of Disciplines: 5 (swimming, diving, water polo, artistic swimming, marathon swimming).

Number of Events: 35 (17 for men, 17 for women, and one mixed event).

Country with Most Olympic Gold Medals: USA (315).

events—the U.S. and Germany. (USA won gold in both events.)

Artistic swimming for women was introduced at the 1984 Olympics in Los Angeles, CA. At Paris 2024, men will compete in artistic swimming for the first time.

Finally, the two **marathon swimming** events are scheduled to be held in the Seine River in Paris. But here's a problem. Swimming in the Seine has been banned since 1923. Why? Because of, well, *pollution*. The French government is working to improve the water quality before the big events.

Olympic Fun Fact

In 1896, the four swimming events were held in the Mediterranean Sea.

Archery

The first modern Olympics were held in Greece in 1896. The games included nine events. Archery was not one of them.

But four years later, in Paris, France, archery was featured for the first time at a modern Olympics. It was included again in 1904, 1908, and 1920.

Then, something strange happened. For the next 52 years—and ten different Olympics—archery was not included on the program.

Finally, in 1972, the archery competition reappeared at the summer Olympics in Munich, Germany. It has been on the program ever since.

2024 Olympic Archery At a Glance

Olympic Debut: 1900, Paris (men's); 1904, St. Louis, MO (women's).

Number of Disciplines: 1 (target archery with recurve bows).

Number of Events: 5 (men's and women's individual and team events and a mixed team event).

Competitors: 128 (64 men, 64 women).

Dates: July 25-August 4.

Country with Most Olympic Gold Medals: Republic of Korea (27).

At Paris 2024, 128 archers (64 men and 64 women) will compete across five events—individual (men and women), and team (men, women, and mixed team).

Only one archer (a man from the USA) has won a gold medal in the individual event twice—once in 1976 and again in 1984. Will someone beat that record at Paris 2024?

Did You Know?

At the 1972 Olympics, archers competed at several different distances from 30 meters to 90 meters.

But today the standard distance for all events is 70 meters (about 77 yards). How far is that? About the length of three tennis courts laid end to end.

Athletics

The ancient Olympic Games took place in Athens, Greece, every four years for almost twelve centuries — from 776BC to at least 393AD. One of the main sports back then— in addition to chariot racing—was athletics. It included a variety of running, jumping, throwing, and walking events.

At the 2024 Olympics, the athletics competition will also include a variety of running, jumping, throwing, and walking events. But there's one big difference.

At the ancient athletics competition, women weren't allowed to compete. In fact, they weren't even allowed to watch the games.

2024 Olympic Athletics At a Glance

Olympic Debut: 1896, Athens, Greece.

Number of Disciplines: 3 (track and field, road running, race walking).

Number of Events: 48.

Competitors: 1,810.

Dates: August 1-11.

Country with Most Olympic Gold Medals: USA (344).

But at the 2024 Olympics, women will compete in all the same events as men—from the 5000m track event to the javelin throw to the 20km Race Walk—a total of 48 events in all.

One athletic event that is slightly different for men and women is the heptathlon (women) and decathlon (men). The women's heptathlon consists of seven events over two days. The men's decathlon consists of ten events over two days.

Did You Know?

Who are the fastest two people on Earth?

Short answer: Whoever wins the 100-meter sprint races at the Olympics.

The winners of the 100-meter race are often considered the fastest people in the world.

Badminton

Birdies, rallies, smashes— they're all in a game of badminton, the fastest racquet sport in the world. Yes, even faster than tennis. Shuttles (or shuttlecocks) can reach speeds of over 321 km/h (200 mph)! The fastest recorded tennis serve was "only" 253.0 km/h (157.2 mph).

The game of badminton got its start one hundred fifty years ago in England. An English duke brought a version of the game—called "Poona"—back from his trip to India.

The game became hugely popular, but it didn't make it to the Olympics until 1992 in Barcelona, Spain. Both men and women competed in singles and doubles matches at those games.

2024 Olympic Badminton At a Glance

Olympic Debut: 1992, Barcelona, Spain.

Number of Events: 5 (singles men and women; doubles men and women; doubles mixed).

Competitors: 172 (86 men, 86 women).

Dates: July 27-August 5.

Country with Most Olympic Gold Medals: China (20).

Today, many people compare a game of badminton to a game of chess. Why? They say that—just like in chess—badminton players must anticipate (or correctly guess) the moves of their opponents.

At the 2024 Summer Olympics in Paris, a total of 172 badminton players (half men half women) will compete for the coveted gold.

What country will end up with the gold? It's anyone's guess. But here's a hint: Athletes from Asian countries have won more Olympic medals in badminton than any others—106 of the 121 medals in Olympic history.

Who Knew?

An official badminton shuttlecock is made with 16 feathers from a goose—all from the left side of the goose only.

Basketball

Basketball was invented in 1891 by a physical education teacher teacher in Springfield, Massachusetts, The popularity of the game grew instantly in both high school and college. By 1898, the first professional league was formed.

But as popular as it was, basketball didn't become an official Olympic sport until 1936 at the Summer Games in Berlin, Germany.

And it took even longer—much longer—for women's basketball to be included on an Olympics program. It made its debut at the 1976 Montreal games, forty years after men's basketball was contested at an Olympics. Yet, most of the rules invented back in 1891 still apply to today's basketball games.

In the late 1980s, a variation of basketball was created. It was played with three players on each team on a half-court setup with one hoop and backboard. It became known as 3x3 basketball and made its Olympic debut at Tokyo 2020.

At Paris 2024, there will be four tournaments: 5-on-5 basketball for men and women, and the 3x3 competition for men and women.

There is one thing constant about these tournaments. Most of the rules invented back in 1891 still apply to today's basketball games.

Did You Know?

Basketball was originally played with peach baskets. After a player scored, someone had to get the ball out of the peach basket by hand.

Boxing

Boxing made its debut at the modern Olympic Games in 1904 in St. Louis, Missouri, USA. And it has been contested at every Summer Games since—except for one.

Boxing was not contested at the 1912 Olympics in Stockholm, Sweden. Why? At the time, a Swedish law banned the sport.

Over the years, the biggest change in boxing events has been in the number of weight classes.

For Paris 2024, the boxing program will include seven weight categories for men and six weight categories for women.

But there have been at least four other major changes in Olympic boxing since 1904.

2024 Olympic Boxing At a Glance

Olympic Debut: 1904, St. Louis, MO (men's); 2012, London, England (women's).

Number of Events: 13.

Number of Competitors: 248.

Dates: July 27-August 10.

Country with Most Olympic Gold Medals: USA (50).

At the 1984 Olympics in Los Angeles, headguards for men were required. The requirement was dropped by Rio 2016, but it is still required for women's boxing.

At London 2012, women's boxing was first introduced.

And at Rio 2016, professional boxers were admitted to the Games, rather than just amateurs.

As of Tokyo 2020, the USA holds the most gold medals in Olympic boxing. Will it add more in 2024?

Did You Know?

At the boxing events at the 1904 Olympics in St. Louis, Missouri, the United States won all the medals. Pretty impressive, right? Well, except for one thing. The U.S. was the only country to compete in boxing events that year.

Breaking

It all started on the streets of the Bronx in New York City in the 1970s. Young people created dance contests that combined dance creativity with amazing athleticism. They called it breaking.

It has taken decades for breaking (often incorrectly called break-dancing) to make it to the Olympics.

But at Paris 2024, breaking will make its official debut. It's the only new sport added to the program for 2024. (Two other sports that were added to the 2020 Olympics in Tokyo—karate and baseball/softball—have both been dropped from the 2024 Olympic program.)

2024 Olympic Breaking At a Glance

Olympic Debut: 2024, Paris, France.

Number of Events: 2 (one for men and one for women).

Number of Competitors: 32 (16 B-Boys and 16 B-Girls).

Dates: August 9-10.

Country with Most Olympic Gold Medals: To come.

What will it take to bring home the gold? Amazing power moves, for sure. Jaw-dropping windmills and freezes, of course. And both a creative and athletic performance often set to funk, rap, and soul music.

This amazing art form is sure to be one of the most popular events at Paris 2024.

Breaking Vocabulary

Breaker: A breaking athlete.

Power Move: A dynamic move or trick that involves breathtaking twists and turns, ending in a freeze.

The Freeze: When a breaker holds his or her body in place for a few seconds in an upside-down position.

Windmill: A power move where a dancer rolls his or her body in a constant circular motion on the floor.

Canoeing

In the canoeing competition at the Olympics, there are two disciplines: canoe sprint and canoe slalom.

In **canoe sprint** events, competitors race on a flatwater course. **In canoe slalom** competitors race a whitewater course.

In both disciplines, athletes race in two types of boats: canoes and kayaks. So, what's the difference?

In canoes, one or two canoers kneel in their boat and use a single-blade paddle. In kayaks, one, two, or four kayakers are seated and use a double-bladed paddle.

At Paris 2024, there will be 10 races in canoe sprint—two canoe and three kayak races each for men and w...

2024 Olympic Canoeing At a Glance

Olympic Debut: 1936, Berlin (canoe sprint); 1972, Munich (canoe slalom).

Number of Disciplines: 2 (canoe-kayak sprint; canoe-kayak slalom).

Number of Events: 16 (10 canoe sprint; six canoe slalom).

Number of Competitors: 199.

Dates: July 27-August 5 (slalom); August 6-10 (sprint).

Country with Most Olympic Gold Medals: Germany (38).

In canoe slalom, there will be six slalom events: Canoe slalom for men and women; kayak slalom for men and women; and extreme kayak (called X-1), a new event for 2024.

Women and Canoeing At the Olympics

Women competed in canoe sprint-kayak competition for the first time in 1948 at the London Olympics. But it wasn't until Tokyo 2020 that women raced for medals in both canoes and kayaks in canoe sprint competition.

At the 1992 Olympics in Barcelona, both men and women competed in kayak slalom. But it wasn't until Tokyo 2020 that women competed in canoe slalom, as well as kayak slalom.

Cycling

What do you think is the most dangerous sport at the Olympics? Gymnastics? Boxing? Table tennis? (Okay, we're just kidding about table tennis.)

Gymnastics and boxing definitely have their share of injuries.. But according to most reports, the most dangerous sport at the Olympics is BMX racing—one of the five disciplines in the sport of cycling.

Road cycling and track cycling for men have been part of the Olympic program since 1896. Cycling events for women were not added to the program for almost one hundred years: road cycling: 1984 and track cycling in 1988.

Mountain bike cycling for men and women was added in 1996, while

BMX racing 2008. Finally, BMX Freestyle Cycling was added in 2020.

At Paris 2024, 514 athletes (half men, half women) will compete in the 22 cycling events.

2024 Olympic Cycling
At a Glance

Olympic Debut: Road cycling, 1896; track cycling, 1896; mountain bike cycling, 1996; BMX racing, 2008; BMX freestyle, 2020.

☐**Number of Disciplines**: 5 (Road Cycling, Track Cycling, Mountain Biking, BMX Racing, and BMX Freestyle).

Number of Events: 22.

Competitors: 514.

Dates: July 27-August 11.

Country with Most Olympic Gold Medals: France (41).

A Quick Look at the
5 Disciplines of Cycling

Road cycling: mass races usually on paved roads.

Track cycling: racing on an oval track.

Mountain bike cycling: racing off-road on very hilly terrain.

BMX racing: competing at high-speed side-by-side over ramps with jumps and turns around tight corners.

BMX freestyle: performing a series of tricks on flat ground, and/or on ramps.

Equestrian

Equestrian events at the Olympics are unique in many ways. One of the most obvious is that the sport is the only one in the Olympic program that involves animals.

But equestrian events at the Olympics are also unique in another way. It's also one of the two Olympic sports where women compete with men equally. (The other sport is sailing.)

At the 1900 Olympics, five equestrian events were contested. Three were jumping events and two were driving events.

By the 1912 Olympics in Stockholm, Sweden, those original five equestrian events were dropped. Instead, dressage, jumping, and eventing made their

official Olympic debut. They have been featured ever since.

At first, the three disciplines were for men only. But, slowly, women were allowed to compete in the three disciplines: dressage in 1952, jumping in 1956, eventing in 1964.

At Paris 2024, 200 riders will compete across three disciplines in six events for both individuals and teams.

Equestrian Vocabulary

Jumping: Riders and horses are timed as they jump over obstacles.

Dressage: Riders and horses perform in a series of movements to music.

Eventing: Combines jumping and dressage with cross-country.

Fencing

Fencing is one of only five sports that has appeared on every Olympics program since 1896. The other four include athletics, cycling, gymnastics, and swimming (one of five disciplines in aquatics).

At first, like almost all other Olympic events, it was a "men only" sport. But in 1924 at the VIII Olympiad in Paris, France, women's fencing entered the Summer Games.

Today, men and women compete in individual and team events using the three types of weapons:

Foil: a light thrusting weapon;

Épée: a heavy thrusting weapon;
Sabre: a light cutting and thrusting weapon.

2024 Olympic Fencing At a Glance

Olympic Debut: 1896, Athens.

Number of Disciplines: 3 (the foil, the épée, and the sabre).

Number of Events: 12 (Individual women's and men's) in each of the three disciplines; Team women's and men's in each of the three disciplines.

Competitors: 212.

Dates: July 27-August 4.

Country with Most Olympic Gold Medals: Italy (49).

At Paris 2024, 212 fencers (half men, half women) will compete in twelve medal events.

Did You Know?

Have you ever wondered why fencers wear white?

The answer is, well, a bit bloody. You see, hundreds of years ago, fencers would fight a duel until one fencer managed to draw blood on his opponent. Since the color white would show blood right away, it was the chosen color of fencing.

Today, of course, it is no longer necessary to "draw blood" to determine a winner. Judges see hits or touches electronically.

But tradition is tradition. And even though the white uniform is no longer required, it is the generally accepted uniform of fencing.

Field Hockey

Hockey is the second most played sport in the world (after football/ soccer). It's been played by boys and girls, men and women for nearly two hundred years.

Yet, it had a hard time becoming a permanent sport at the Olympics.

It was first held at the 1908 games in London. But it was dropped four years later at the 1912 Olympics in Stockholm, Sweden.

It reappeared at the 1920 Olympics in Antwerp, Belgium, but was omitted again at the 1924 Olympics in Paris.

Finally, in 1928 at the Olympics in Amsterdam, the Netherlands,

2024 Olympic Field Hockey At a Glance

Olympic Debut: 1908, London (men's); 1980, Moscow (women's).

Number of Events: 2 (men, women).

Number of Competitors: Twenty-four teams (twelve each for men and women).

Dates: July 27-August 9.

Country with Most Olympic Gold Medals: India (8).

---

hockey became a permanent sport on the Olympics program.

Of course, it took quite a few more Olympiads before women's hockey was included on an Olympic program. That finally happened at the 1980 Olympics in Moscow.

At the 2024 Olympics, twenty-four teams (12 men's, 12 women's) will battle it out for Olympic gold.

Keep your eye on the men's team from Belgium and the women's team from the Netherlands. They won gold at Tokyo 2020. Can they do it again in Paris?

Did You Know?

Hockey got its name from the French word *hocquet*. A hocquet is a long stick with a hook at one end, known as a crook. It is used by shepherds to manage sheep. The curved shape of a hockey stick looks like a crook or hocquet.

Football

It probably wouldn't surprise you to learn that football (or soccer, as it is called in the U.S.) is both the most popular sport in the world and the world's most played sport.

It also has appeared at all but one Olympiads since its debut at Paris 1900. (It was not included in the Games in the 1932 Olympics in Los Angeles.)

In 1992, at the Olympic Games in Barcelona, a new rule went into effect. To play at the Olympics, competitors had to be under 23 years old.

But in 1996, at the Atlanta Olympics, the rule changed slightly. The new rule said a maximum of three players per squad could be over 23 years old.

> ### 2024 Olympic Football At a Glance
>
> **Olympic Debut**: 1900, Paris (men's); 1996, Atlanta (women's)
> **Number of Events**: 2 (1 men, 1 women)
> **Number of Competitors**: 504
> **Dates**: July 24-August 10
> **Country with Most Olympic Gold Medals:** USA (4).

At Atlanta 1996, women's football finally made its Olympic debut. Canada won their first gold medal in women's football that year by defeating Sweden 3-2. Will they make it back-to back gold medals in 2024?

Did You Know?

When it comes to football at the Olympics, what do Great Britain, Uruguay, Hungary, Argentina, and Brazil have in common?

Answer: They are the only five countries to win back-to-back gold medals in men's football at the Olympics:

Great Britain, 1908 and 1912; Uruguay, 1924 and 1928; Hungary, 1964 and 1968; Argentina, 2004 and 2008 Olympics; and Brazil, 2016 and 2020 Olympics

In women's football at the Olympics, USA won "back-to-back-to-back" gold medals in Athens 2004, Beijing 2008, and London 2012.

Golf

At the Games of the II Olympiad in 1900 in Paris, women were allowed to compete in only five sports: golf, equestrianism, sailing, croquet, and tennis. Out of a total of 997 athletes at those Games, only twenty-two were women.

But three of those women made history during the very long Olympiad. (The games took place between May 14 and October 28.)

The first woman to make history at that Olympiad was Hélène de Pourtalès. She was an American born sailor, representing Switzerland. She and her crew won a gold medal in a sailing event in May. That made her the first woman to win a gold medal in a *team* event at the Olympics.

2024 Olympic Golf At a Glance

Olympic Debut: 1900, Paris.
Number of Events: 2.
Number of Competitors: 120 (60 men, 60 women).
Dates: August 1-4 (men); August 7-10 (women).
Country with Most Olympic Gold Medals: USA (5).

The second woman to make history during the 1900 games was Charlotte Cooper from Great Britain. In July at the age of 19, she won gold in the women's singles tennis competition. That made her the first female *individual* champion in Olympic history.

The third woman to make history at the 1900 Olympics was an American golfer named Margaret Abbott. In October 1900, she became the first female *American* to win gold at an Olympic event.

At the 2024 Olympics, women will make history again. For the first at an Olympics, there will be the same number of female and male athletes *and* the same number of events for both. That gives everyone the same opportunity to take home gold, silver, and bronze medals.

23

Gymnastics

Gymnastics was introduced at the very first Olympic Games of the modern era in 1896 and has been included in every edition since.

At first, only men participated in gymnastic events. No surprise there, right?

But in the 1928 Games in Amsterdam, women joined the program for the first time.

Since then, gymnastics events have changed a lot. For example, rope climbing was part of the gymnastics events in 1896, 1904, 1924, and 1932. But it has not been on an Olympics program since.

2024 Olympic Gymnastics At a Glance

Olympic Debut: 1896, Athens.

Number of Disciplines: 3 (artistic gymnastics, rhythmic gymnastics, trampoline).

Number of Events: 18. (Artistic:14, Rhythmic: 2, Trampoline: 2).

Competitors: 318 (110 men, 206 women).

Dates: Artistic: July 27-August 5; Rhythmic: August 8-10; Trampoline: August 2.

Country with Most Olympic Gold Medals: Soviet Union (73).

Today, there are three sports that make up the Olympic gymnastics program— artistic gymnastics, rhythmic gymnastics, and trampoline.

Artistic Gymnastics (since 1896): In this discipline, athletes compete on different apparatus and floor routines.

Rhythmic Gymnastics (since 1984): Athletes perform on a floor with either a ball hoop, clubs, ribbon, or rope.

Trampoline (since 2000): Athletes perform acrobatic movements such as twists and somersaults, while bouncing on a trampoline. It became a gymnastic discipline in 2000.

Handball

Imagine football, basketball **and water polo** all rolled into one new sport.

Actually, you don't have to imagine it. Simply watch a fast-paced game of handball—the fastest team sport at the Summer Games.

The game is thought to be one of the oldest sports in the world. A form of handball was played by the Greeks back in the 5th century BC.

Yet, the basic rules of the game haven't changed much in centuries. Two teams compete to throw a ball into the opposing team's goal.

Field handball made its first (and only) appearance as an Olympic sport at the 1936 Games in Berlin, Germany. But then it didn't appear

on an Olympic program again for almost four decades.

At the 1972 Olympics in Munich, Germany, handball made its comeback—this time as an indoor sport.

Four years later, women's handball was introduced at the 1976 Olympics in Montreal, Canada. Both men's and women's handball have been contested at the Summer Olympics ever since.

Judo

It probably won't come as a surprise to learn that Japan has won three times as many gold medals in Judo as the second-place record holder. After all, Judo was invented in Japan in 1882 as a martial art. It emphasizes physical fitness, mental discipline, and sportsmanship.

It took almost one hundred years for Judo to become an Olympic sport. But in 1964 at the summer games in (appropriately) Tokyo, Japan, judo made its Olympic debut.

But then at the very next Olympic games, it was dropped. Fortunately, in 1972, judo returned. It's been an Olympic sport ever since.

At first, only male "judoka" participated in the sport. But in 1992 at the Barcelona, Spain, games,

2024 Olympic Judo At a Glance

Olympic Debut: 1964, Tokyo, Japan (male judoka); 1992, Barcelona, Spain (female judoka).

Number of Events: 15 (seven weight classes for men, seven for women, plus a mixed team tournament).

Competitors: 372 (186 men, 186 women).

Dates: July 27-August 3.

Country with Most Olympic Gold Medals: Japan (48).

women judoka competed for the first time.

At Paris 2024, judokas will greet each other at the beginning of a match with a bow, as is the custom. It's a way of saying, "I will play by the rules." Those rules include fair play and safety.

Then, during a match, each judoka will strive for points based on throws, holds, and submissions.

Olympic Quick Quiz

What does "judo" mean in Japanese?

(a) Shoulder throw

(b) Gentle way

(c) White uniform

Answer: (b) Gentle way.

Modern Pentathlon

The original pentathlon at the ancient Olympics consisted of five disciplines: running, jumping, spear-throwing (or javelin), discus, and wrestling. It was the climax (or last contest) of the Games in Ancient Greece.

The modern pentathlon also includes five disciplines that are said to test the strengths of a "complete" athlete. The modern pentathlon consists of pistol shooting, épée fencing, freestyle swimming, equestrian show jumping, and cross country running.

The event was first held for men at the 1912 Olympic Games in Stockholm, Sweden. It's been on the Olympic program for men ever since.

At the Summer Games in Sydney,

> ## 2024 Olympic Modern Pentathlon At a Glance
>
> **Olympic Debut**: 1912, Stockholm (men's events); 2000, Sydney (women's event).
>
> **Number of Disciples**: 5 (swimming, fencing, equestrian jumping, and running and pistol shooting).
>
> **Number of Events**: 2 (one for men and another for women).
>
> **Number of Competitors**: 72 (36 men, 36 women).
>
> **Dates**: August 8-11.
>
> **Country with Most Olympic Gold Medals**: (tie) Sweden and Hungary (each 9).

Australia, in 2000, women were allowed to compete in the modern pentathlon for the first time.

At London 2012, the events changed slightly. There were still separate events for fencing, swimming, and equestrian. But pistol shooting and running were combined into what is now known as the laser run.

> ### Did You Know?
>
> **At London 2012,** laser guns were used for the first time in the modern pentathlon, instead of lead-firing pistols. The decision to use laser guns was made both for safety and for the environment.

Rowing

Rowing events have been **staged** at the Olympics almost since the beginning of the modern era in 1896. Almost.

Unfortunately, even though rowing events were scheduled for the 1896 games, they didn't take place. Why?

The competition was scheduled to take place at sea. But, at the last minute the competition had to be cancelled due to bad weather and high winds.

So, the first Olympic rowing champions didn't take their place on the podium until four years later at the second modern Games in Paris in 1900. They were all men.

Finally, at the 1976 Olympics in Montreal, Canada, women were allowed to compete in rowing.

2024 Olympic Rowing At a Glance

Olympic Debut: 1900, Paris (men's events); 1976, Montreal (women's events)

Number of Disciplines: 2 (double scull and sweep rowing).

Number of Events: 14 (seven each for men and women).

Number of Competitors: 502.

Dates: July 27-August 3

Country with Most Olympic Gold Medals: (tie) USA and E. Germany (each 33).

At the 2024 Olympics, 506 athletes will compete in double scull and sweep rowing. In sweep rowing events, rowers hold a single oar with both hands. In double scull, rowers hold one oar in both hands.

Olympics Fun Fact

At the 1928 Summer Olympics in Amsterdam, one of the rowers stopped rowing for a moment for an unusual reason. What was it?

a. An alligator was in the water.

b. His boat began leaking.

c. Baby ducks swam into his lane.

Answer: C
A family of baby ducks swam into the rower's lane. So, he stopped rowing for a moment to let them pass. Fortunately, he still won the gold.

Rugby Sevens

First, there was Rugby Union, a 15-a-side game invented in 1823 at Rugby School in Great Britain.

Later, in 1883, rugby sevens was invented. And, as the name suggests, it's a seven-a-side game.

Rugby Union was featured at the Olympics four times—at Paris 1900, London 1908, Antwerp 1920, and Paris 1924.

Surprisingly, it was then dropped as an Olympic sport. It wasn't brought back until the 2016 Summer Olympics in Rio de Janeiro.

But it came back as Rugby Sevens. Separate tournaments for men and women were held. At Paris 2024, twenty-four teams (twelve for men and twelve for women) once again

2024 Olympic Rugby Sevens At a Glance

Olympic Debut: 1900, Paris, Rugby Union; 2016, Rio, Rugby Sevens.

Number of Events: 2.

Number of Competitors: 312.

Dates: July 24-30.

Country with Most Olympic Gold Medals: Fiji (2).

---

compete in the men's and women's tournaments.

In both the 2016 and 2020 Games, the tiny country of Fiji took home the gold in the men's tournament. Can they make it three in a row?

Rugby and American Football

What's the Difference?

Rugby and its American cousin football are alike in many ways. For example, both sports use an oval-shaped ball. Both sports also advance the ball into the opponent's end zone, known as a *touchdown* in American football, and a *try* in rugby.

But they are also different in many ways. For example, in American football, a tackle ends a play, but not in rugby.

Perhaps the biggest difference, though, is what players wear. American football players are required to wear helmets and shoulder, body and leg padding. In rugby there is no mandatory protection.

Sailing

Sailing contests were supposed to take place at the first Olympic Games of the modern era in 1896. However, bad weather and high winds forced the events to be canceled.

But at the II Olympiad in Paris in 1900, history was made. An American-born woman named Hélène de Pourtalès competed with her husband and brother in a team sailing event. And they won!

That made Hélène de Pourtalès the first woman to win a gold medal at the Olympics.

Since that historic event, sailing has been a part of the Olympic program at every Olympiad except

1904. At all those early Summer Olympics, women competed in teams with men. The first women's only event in sailing wasn't introduced until the Summer Games in Seoul, South Korea, in 1988.

At Paris 2024, 330 sailors (half men, half women) will compete across ten events, including a new event for 2024–kitesurfing.

Did You Know?

Women competed for the first time at the 1900 Olympics in Paris. Of a total of 997 athletes, only twenty-two were women. They competed in five sports: tennis, sailing, croquet, equestrianism, and golf.

Since then, women's events in various sports have been added very slowly over the many Olympiads. Finally, at Paris 2024, there will be the same number of female athletes as males at the games for the first time ever.

Shooting

The USA has won more medals in shooting events at the Olympics than any other country. In fact, it's won more than twice as many gold medals in shooting than its nearest rival (China).

Shooting has been part of the Olympics since 1896. In fact, it was one of only nine official sports contested at that first modern Olympics.

Since then, shooting has been contested at every Olympics except two. (It was not included in the 1904 or 1928 Olympic Games.)

Women made their Olympic debut in shooting at the 1968 Olympics in Mexico City. But it wasn't until eight years later—at Montreal 1976–that a woman won a medal in Olympic shooting.

2024 Olympic Shooting At a Glance

Olympic Debut: 1896, Athens.

Number of Disciplines: 3 (rifle, pistol, and shotgun).

Number of Events: 15.

Number of Competitors: 340 (170 men, 170 women).

Dates: July 27-August 5.

Country with Most Olympic Gold Medals in Shooting: USA (57).

Margaret Murdock from the U.S. won a silver medal in Rifle Three Positions. In this event, athletes compete in three positions (prone, kneeling, standing).

At Paris 2024, 300 athletes from more than 100 countries will compete across fifteen events in three different disciplines: rifle, pistol, and shotgun.

Rifle and pistol events take place on shooting ranges with targets at distances up to 50 m. Shotgun events take place outdoors. Competitors shoot at flying targets.

Father of Modern Olympic Games

Pierre de Coubertin is known as the father of the modern Olympic Games. He was also a pistol champion. That may be why he wanted shooting to be an event at the first Olympic games in 1896.

Skateboarding

What do you do when you want to "ride the waves," but there are no waves around?

Answer: Try "sidewalk surfing," as it was once known or skateboarding as it will be contested for the second time in Olympic history at Paris 2024.

The exciting competition will take place in two locations:

Park competition takes place in a "bowl" with steep sides and obstacles. Skateboarders perform a variety of mid-air tricks.

Street events take place on a city "street-like" course. The course includes everything from stairs and handrails to benches and curbs. Skateboarders use these obstacles to perform their tricks.

2024 Olympic Skateboarding At a Glance

Olympic Debut: 2020, Tokyo, Japan☐.
Number of Disciplines: 2 (street and park).
Number of Events: 4 (street, men and women, and park, men and women).
Competitors: 88.
Dates: July 27-August 7.
Country with Most Olympic Gold Medals: Japan (3).

At Paris 2024, a total of 88 skateboarders will compete in four medal events—street and park, each for men and women.

At Tokyo 2020, the USA women's team missed out on a medal. But the men's team brought home a bronze medal in Park and Street.

Can they add to their medal count at Paris 2024?

A Bit of Olympic History

Between 1896 and 2020, the Summer Olympic Games have been *scheduled* thirty-two times. But the Games have only been contested twenty-nine times. Why?

The games were cancelled on three different occasions—in 1916 because of World War I and in 1940 and 1944 because of World War II.

Sport Climbing

Power, endurance, speed, and even a little problem solving: Those are just some of the skills you need to be a gold medal winner in sport climbing at the Olympics.

The sport made its Olympic debut in Tokyo four years ago. At those Games, athletes competed in a single event that combined three disciplines: boulder, lead, and speed. The athlete with the lowest combined score for all three events took home the gold.

In Paris 2024 there will be two disciplines contested: speed (for men and for women), and boulder and lead combined (also for men and for women).

A total 68 athletes will compete for gold in the two disciplines: 28 for speed and 40 for boulder-and-lead.

2024 Olympic Sport Climbing At a Glance

Olympic Debut: 2020, Tokyo, Japan.

Number of Disciplines: 2 (boulder and lead combined, and speed).

Number of Events: 4 (boulder and lead combined, women's and men's; speed, women's and men's).

Competitors: 68 (28 for speed and 40 for boulder and lead).

Dates: August 5-10.

Country with Most Olympic Gold Medals: (tie) Slovenia and Spain (each 1).

So. what's the difference between the two disciplines?

In Speed, two athletes complete for the fastest time in a climb up a 15-meter-high wall.

In boulder and lead combined, boulder athletes climb 4.5m high walls without ropes, in a four-minutes time period.

In the lead event, athletes climb with a rope as high as they can on a wall over 15m high in six minutes.

A Bit of Olympic History

In the history of the Summer Olympics, the USA has hosted the Games more than any other country—four times in 1904 in St. Louis, 1932 in Los Angeles, 1984 in Los Angeles, and 1996 in Atlanta. The 2028 Games are also scheduled for Los Angeles.

Surfing

In the 1920s, a Hawaiian athlete named Duke Kahanamoku —a five-time Olympic medalist in swimming—began a campaign to make surfing an Olympic sport.

It took nearly one hundred years for Duke (and others) to achieve that goal. But in 2020 at the XXXII Olympiad in Tokyo, Japan, surfing finally made it onto the Olympic program.

The sport will be contested for the second time at Paris 2024. But the surfing competition won't be taking place *in* Paris. (No water, no surf.)

Instead, the surfing events at Paris 2024 will take place in Tahiti, an island in French Polynesia. Waves

**2024 Olympic Surfing
At a Glance**

Olympic Debut: 2020, Tokyo, Japan. ☐
Number of Events: 2 (shortboard for men and women).
Competitors: 48 (24 for each gender).
Dates: July 27-August 5.
Country with Most Olympic Gold Medals: (tie) Brazil, USA (each 1).

there often reach up to 3m (9.8 ft.) high.

Tahiti is 15,771 kilometers (9,800 miles) away from the host city. That may seem strange. But this is not the first time that has happened.

At the 1956 Olympics in Melbourne, Australia, the equestrian events were held in Stockholm, Sweden—some 15,610 kilometers (9,700 miles) away from Melbourne.

At Paris 2024, twenty-four men and twenty-four women will compete in the surfing competition at Teahupo'o Beach—undoubtedly the perfect location for speed, power, and amazing surfing tricks.

Mother, May I

Surfing competition has its own set of rules for how to surf "politely." For example, only one surfer can ride a wave at a time. The surfer closest to the peak of a big wave has the right of way.

Table Tennis

What does it take to become a medal contender in table tennis at the Olympic games?

Many professionals say it can take up to 10,000 hours of serious practice. 10,000 hours! That's twenty hours a week, every week, for ten years.

Table tennis made its Olympic debut in Seoul 1988 with men's and women's singles and doubles.

Since then, one country has dominated the sport. The People's Republic of China! In fact, China has won 32 of 37 gold medals from 1988 to 2021.

Table Tennis is a fast sport. How fast? A really good table tennis player will slap the ball across the table at 100 mph (160 km/h). By comparison, the average speed of a major league fastball is 93 mph (149.6 km/h).

At Paris 2024, a total of 172 table tennis players (half men, half women) will compete across five events (two per gender and a mixed).

The U.S. has not yet won a medal in table tennis at any Summer Olympic Games. Will that change at Paris 2024?

2024 Olympic Table Tennis At a Glance

Olympic Debut: ☐ 1988 Seoul.

Number of Events: 5 (two per gender and a mixed).

Competitors: 172 (half men, half women).

Dates: July 27-August 10.

Country with Most Olympic Gold Medals: China (32).

Table Tennis "Back Then"

Table tennis was invented in England in the 1880s. But back then, it was a little different than it is today. How? There are at least three ways:

(1) The "net" was a line of books on a table.

(2) The ball was the rounded top of a champagne cork

(3) And the paddle? Often it was simply a cigar box lid.

All sounds pretty creative, right?

Taekwondo

Taekwondo is one of only three martial arts ever competed at the Olympics. Judo is the second. And karate is a third. (But karate was contested only once—at Tokyo 2020. It will not be contested at the 2024 or 2028 Olympics.)

The word "taekwondo" is a Korean word. That should not be surprising. The martial art was created in Korea in the early 1940s, not Japan, as many people think. Today, it is Korea's national sport.

The word is made up of three parts: "tae," which means to destroy with the feet: "kwon," which means to fight or strike; and "do," which means "way." The word can be translated to mean "the way of kicking and punching."

**2024 Olympic Taekwondo
At a Glance**

Olympic Debut: 2000, Sydney, Australia.

Number of Events: 8 (across different weight categories).

Competitors: 128 (64 men and 64 women).

Dates: August 7-10.

Country with Most Olympic Gold Medals: Republic of Korea (12).

This martial art became an official Olympic sport in 2000 at the Sydney, Australia, summer games. Unlike many other sports, at its debut, there were events for both men and women.

At Paris 2024, 128 athletes (64 men and 64 women) will compete in the taekwondo competition across eight different weight categories (four per gender).

Who will bring home the gold? That's anyone's guess. But be sure to watch for fast, powerful spinning kicks. They are rewarded with extra points.

Did You Know?

At Tokyo 2020, history was made when an American woman won a gold medal for the first time in taekwondo.

Tennis

Tennis was one of the nine sports played at the first modern Olympics in Athens in 1896. But only two tournaments were played: men's singles and men's doubles.

Four years later, at the Olympic Games in Paris, France, women were allowed to compete in both singles and mixed doubles.

However, after the 1924 Games in Antwerp, Belgium, tennis was dropped from the program. It didn't return for sixty-four years but finally made a come back to the Olympic Games in 1988.

Since then, it has become one of the most popular sports at the Summer Olympics.

At Paris 2024, 172 players will compete for a medal in five tennis

2024 Olympic Tennis
At a Glance

Olympic Debut: 1896, Athens, Greece☐ (men); 1900, Paris, France (women).

Number of Events: 5 (singles, men and women; doubles, men and women; and mixed doubles).

Competitors: 172.

Dates: July 27-August 4.

Country with Most Olympic Gold Medals: USA (21).

events—men's singles, women's singles, men's doubles, women's doubles, and mixed doubles. Who will take home the gold? Stay tuned.

A Golden Slam

Every year, there are four Grand Slam tennis tournaments around the world—the Australian Open, the French Open, Wimbledon, and the US Open. For anyone to win all four in a single year is a pretty amazing accomplishment. In fact, only five players in the history of tennis have ever achieved that goal.

But there is an even bigger achievement in tennis. That's the Golden Slam. What's that?

If a player wins an Olympic gold medal in tennis *and* all four Grand Slam events in the same year, he or she is said to have won a Golden Slam. How many have achieved that status? Only one. That was the legendary German player, Steffi Graff, in 1988.

Triathlon

The Triathlon—an Olympic sport that includes swimming, cycling, and running—sounds like an event that would have been contested at the very first modern Olympics in 1896.

But here's the strange thing. It's a fairly new sport at the Olympics. It wasn't invented until the early 1970s. And it didn't make its Olympic debut until 2000 at the Summer Olympics in Sydney, Australia.

At the Olympics, both the men's and the women's individual competition consists of three events:

1.5 km swim (close to a mile).

40 km bike ride (about 25 miles).

10 km run (about 6 miles).

2024 Olympic Triathlon At a Glance

Olympic Debut: □2000, Sydney, Australia.

Number of Disciplines: 3 (swimming, cycling, running).

Number of Events: 3 (men, women, mixed relay).

Competitors: 110.

Dates: July 30-31 (men's and women's); August 5 (mixed relay).

Country with Most Olympic Gold Medals: Great Britain (3).

At Tokyo 2020 a mixed relay was added to the program. Each team includes four athletes (two men and two women).

In the mixed relay, each athlete completes a 300m swim, 6.8km cycle, and 2km run in a relay format.

The 2024 Olympics will see 110 men and women compete in one of the most strenuous events in all of the Games.

No "Drafting" Allowed

In cycling, when an athlete rides close behind the rider in front of him, it's called "drafting." It helps the cyclist by reducing wind resistance. There's just one problem. It is not allowed during the cycling part of a triathlon. If you get caught, you can be disqualified.

Volleyball

How about a game of "mintonette"?

"A game of what?" you ask.

Volleyball, of course."

Mintonette" is what it used to be called. The word comes from the game badminton.

The game of mintonette was created in 1895 and got popular real fast. Soon it was known as volleyball.

The sport was played as a "demonstration event" at the 1924 Olympics in Paris, France. But it didn't become an official Olympic medal sport until 1964 at the Olympic Games in Tokyo, Japan. It has been contested at every Summer Games since then.

2024 Olympic Volleyball At a Glance

Olympic Debut: 1964, Volleyball, Tokyo☐, Japan; 1996, Beach Volleyball, Atlanta, Georgia, USA.

Number of Disciplines: 2 (indoor volleyball and beach volleyball).

Number of Events: 4.

Competitors: 24 volleyball teams (12 per gender) and 48 beach volleyball teams (24 per gender).

Dates: July 27-August 11.

Country with the Most Olympic Gold Medals: USA (11).

Beach volleyball became an Olympic sport in 1996. Like indoor volleyball, there were editions for both men and women from the beginning.

At Paris 2024, a total of 24 teams (twelve teams per gender) will participate in indoor volleyball.

A total of 48 teams (twenty-four teams per gender) will participate in the beach volleyball tournament.

So, are you ready for a fast game of mintonette. . .er, volleyball?

Did You Know?

In a game of volleyball, the ball can reach speeds of up to 130km/h (80.7 mph).

Wrestling

Wrestling may very well be the oldest sport in history. In fact, there is evidence that wrestling matches were held as long ago as 3000 BC.

Today, wrestling contests at the Olympics consist of two disciplines: Greco-Roman and Freestyle.

Greco-Roman wrestling was the style of wrestling contested at the first modern Olympics in 1896. It has been contested at every Summer Olympics since 1896 (except Paris 1900).

Freestyle wrestling was added to the Olympic program in 1904. It has been contested at the Summer Olympics ever since.

What's the difference between the two styles of wrestling? Greco-Roman wrestlers can only hold their opponents above the waist. Freestyle

2024 Olympic Wrestling At a Glance

Olympic Debut: 1896, Athens (Greco-Roman style); 1904, St. Louis, MO (freestyle wrestling).

Number of Disciplines: 2 (Freestyle and Greco-Roman).

Number of Events: 18 (6 events for men, freestyle; 6 events for men, Greco-Roman; 6 events for women, freestyle).

Competitors: 288.

Dates: August 5-12.

Country with Most Olympic Gold Medals: Soviet Union (62).

---

wrestlers can attack any part of their opponent's body.

At the 2004 Summer Olympics in Athens, Greece, women's freestyle wrestling was added to the program.

At Paris 2024, 288 wrestlers (men and women) will compete across eighteen different weight categories. Men will wrestle each other in both freestyle and Greco-Roman. Women will wrestle each other only in freestyle wrestling.

Did You Know?

There are two main ways to win an Olympic wrestling match: pinning an opponent's shoulders to the mat, or winning the most points through different moves, like holds.

Weightlifting

The goal in weightlifting competition is pretty simple: lift more weight than anyone else.

But as simple as it may seem, it's not easy. It takes years of practice — and quite a bit of strength, of course.

Weightlifting was one of the nine sports featured at the very first Olympic Games (of the modern era) in 1896. Back then, there were two weightlifting events: lifting with one hand and lifting with two hands.

After 1896, the weightlifting sport disappeared from the Olympic program in 1900, 1908 and 1912.

Finally, in 1920, weightlifting was reintroduced at the Games in Antwerp, Belgium. And it has been included ever since.

One big addition came at the 2000 Games in Sydney, Australia. Women's competitions were finally added to the weightlifting sport.

At Paris 2024, a total of 120 weightlifters (60 men, 60 women) will compete in ten weight classes (5 for men, 5 for women).

Did You Know?

In each weight division, weightlifters at the Olympics compete in two lifts: the snatch and the clean and jerk:

The snatch involves lifting the weight from the ground to overhead in one motion.

The clean and jerk involves lifting the weight from the ground to the shoulders, then from the shoulders to overhead in two motions.

The Modern Olympics Timeline
At a Glance

1896:   First modern Olympics are held in Olympia, Greece.

American track and field athlete James Connolly becomes the first athlete to win a gold medal (though it was silver at the time) at the first modern Olympic Games. Connolly wins a gold medal in the triple jump (then called the hop, skip, and jump).

1900:   Women are allowed to participate in the Games in Paris, France. Twenty-two women out of a total of 997 athletes compete in five sports: tennis, sailing, croquet, equestrian, and golf.

1904:   Gold, silver, and bronze medals are awarded for the first time at the St. Louis (Missouri) Games. It's also the first time that the United States hosts the summer Olympics.

1920:   The Athletes' Oath is introduced at the Summer Olympic Games.

1924:   Olympics games are separated into summer and winter games held the same calendar year.

1928:   The Olympic Flame is lit for the first time during the opening ceremony of the 1928 Olympic Games in Amsterdam.

1936:   First Olympic Torch Relay takes place between Olympia, Greece, and Berlin, Germany.

1956:   Olympics are held in Melbourne, Australia, the first time the games are held in the Southern Hemisphere.

1980:   Sixty-six nations, including the United States, boycott the 1980 Olympics in Moscow after that country's invasion of Afghanistan in 1979.

1992:   After the 1992 Games in Barcelona, Spain, the summer and winter games alternate every two years, beginning with the winter games in 1994 and the summer games in 1996.

Professionals are allowed to compete in men's basketball. The U.S. "Dream Team" (including Michael Jordan and Larry Bird, and Magic Johnson) wins the gold.

2004:   The Games are held in Athens, Greece, for the first time in 108 years.

2021:   The 2020 Summer Games are held in Tokyo, Japan.

2024:   The Summer Games are scheduled to be held in Paris, France.

Summer Olympic Games: 1896-2024

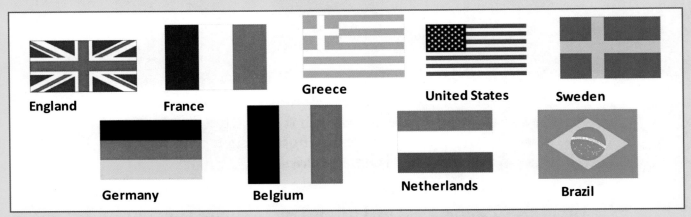

England   France   Greece   United States   Sweden
Germany   Belgium   Netherlands   Brazil

I. 1896, Athens, Greece

II. 1900, Paris, France

III. 1904, St. Louis, Missouri, USA

IV. 1908, London, England

V. 1912, Stockholm, Sweden

VI. 1916, Berlin, Germany: CANCELLED

VII. 1920, Antwerp, Belgium

VIII. 1924, Paris, France

IX. 1928, Amsterdam, Netherlands

X. 1932, Los Angeles, California, USA

XI. 1936, Berlin, Germany

XII. 1940, Tokyo, Japan: CANCELLED

XIII. 1944, London, England: CANCELLED

XIV. 1948, London, England

XV. 1952, Helsinki, Finland

XVI. 1956, Melbourne, Australia

XVII. 1960, Rome, Italy

XVIII. 1964, Tokyo, Japan

XIX. 1968, Mexico City, Mexico

XX. 1972, Munich, Germany

XXI. 1976, Montreal, Canada

XXII. 1980, Moscow, Soviet Union

XXIII. 1984, Los Angeles, California, USA

XXIV. 1988, Seoul, Republic of Korea

XXV. 1992, Barcelona, Spain,

XXVI. 1996, Atlanta, Georgia, USA

XXVII. 2000, Sydney, Australia

XXVIII. 2004, Athens, Greece

XXIX. 2008, Beijing, China

XXX. 2012, London, England

XXXI. 2016, Rio de Janeiro, Brazil

XXXII. 2020, Tokyo, Japan

XXXIII. 2024, Paris, France

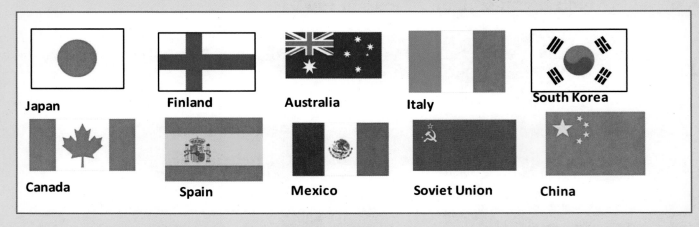

Japan   Finland   Australia   Italy   South Korea
Canada   Spain   Mexico   Soviet Union   China

Explore the World

Find these fun-to-read country books and more on
curiouskidspress.com

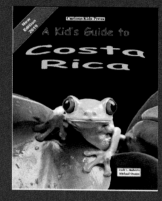

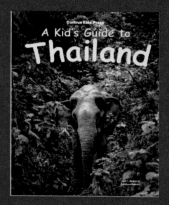

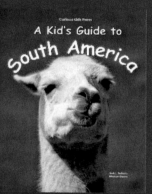

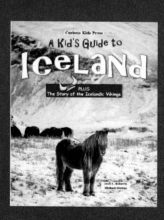

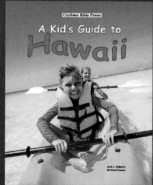
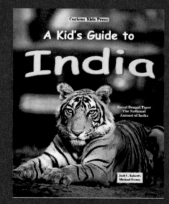

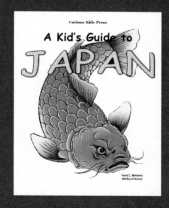

Curious Kids Press
www.curiouskidspress.com

Three Nonfiction Books for Kids

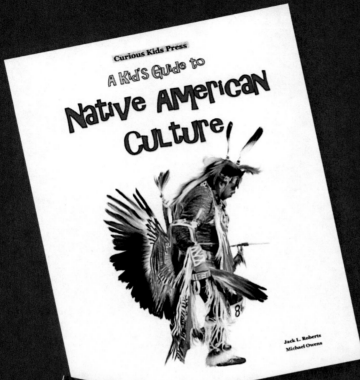

Available on amazon.com

About
Curious Kids Press
For Parents and Teachers

Curious Kids Press (CKP) was founded in 2017 with the goal of providing engaging, easy-to-read books about countries and cultures around the world for young readers. Each book includes colorful photographs, informational charts and graphs, and quirky and bizarre "Did You Know" facts, all designed to bring the country and its people to life. Designed primarily for recreational, high-interest reading, the informational text series is also a great resource for students to use to research geography topics or writing assignments.

In addition to our "country books," CKP has also published several special editions of the "Kid's Guide" series, including *A Kid's Guide to Climate Change*, *A Kid's Guide to Native American Culture*, and *A Kid's Guide to World Religions*, as well as special editions about the winter and summer Olympics.

About the Reading Level

A Kid's Guide to . . . is an informational text series designed for kids in grades 4 to 6, ages 9 to 12. For some young readers, the series will provide new reading challenges based on the vocabulary and sentence structure. For other readers, the series will review and reinforce reading skills already achieved. While for still other readers, the book will match their current skill level, regardless of age or grade level.

About the Authors

Jack L. Roberts began his career in educational publishing at Children's Television Workshop (now Sesame Workshop), where he was Senior Editor of The Sesame Street/Electric Company Reading Kits. Later, at Scholastic Inc., he was the founding editor of a high-interest/low-reading level magazine for middle school students. He also founded two technology magazines for teachers and administrators.

Roberts is the author of more than two dozen biographies and other nonfiction titles for young readers, published by Scholastic Inc., the Lerner Publishing Group, Teacher Created Materials, Benchmark Education, and others.. More recently, he was the co-founder of WordTeasers, an educational series of card decks designed to help kids of all ages improve their vocabulary through "conversation, not memorization."

Michael Owens is a noted jazz dance teacher, award-winning wildlife photographer, graphic arts designer, and devoted animal lover.

In 2017, Roberts and Owens launched Curious Kids Press (CKP), an educational publishing company focused on publishing high-interest, nonfiction books for young readers, primarily books about countries and cultures around the world. Currently, CKP has published two series of country books: "A Kid's Guide to..." (for ages 9-12 and "Let's Visit . . ." (for ages 6-8) — both designed to help young readers explore the wonderful world of diversity in everything from food and holidays to geography and traditions.

Made in the USA
Monee, IL
03 July 2024

61178557R00029